TELLING YOU EVERYTHING

CINDY HOCHMAN

Published by Unleash Press

Book cover design by Christopher Shanahan

Printed in the United States of America

ISBN 978-8-9862743-3-1

This chapbook is dedicated to my beautiful, fearless, and feisty ~~step~~mom, Jean Pearl Keller Sostchen, whose deep love and wisdom have always guided me, and still guide me, and always will.

And in loving memory of Shirley Sostchen, William Sostchen, and Rick Sostchen, and all my Sostchen, Hoffman, and Cooper ancestors, whose DNA I proudly carry.

Credits

Grateful thanks to the editors of the following journals where some of these poems first appeared, sometimes in different versions and/or with different titles:

Arsenic Lobster, Brevitas Anthology, Brownstone Poets Anthology, Chantarelle's Notebook, Clockwise Cat, Concrete Mist Anthology (Heath Brougher, editor), Home Planet News, Kiyi (translated into Turkish by Ali Bilir), Levure Littéraire, Litterateur RW, LiVE Mag!, Möbius (The Poetry Magazine), Muddy River Poetry Review, Paper Teller Diorama (great weather for MEDIA Anthology), Pirene's Fountain Anthology, Redheaded Stepchild, SurVision Magazine, Unbroken Journal, and *Unlikely Stories.*

Contents

Telling You Everything

Be brief and tell us everything.
—Charles Simic

I am all moan and bone and dangling participles. I am all pipes and drums but no voice box. My body is hamstrung and jagged. I am a bellyful of barren. These days I have become nothing but chocolate bars and razor blades.

Cindy Hochman

Gladiatrix

When I wake in the morning
all horsey-faced and *verklempt*
with my samurai sword
and HazMat suit
I take a deep ninja breath
and get ready to swashbuckle
another double-edged daggered day

Leaving the Light On For You

Because you're a poet
and I'm a poet
our mouths can meet
at the edge of the crease
between stanzas
at the last-gasp motel

Cindy Hochman

Infrastructure

I write couplets
though I am not a couple

I write prose because I'm breathless and endless and long-lined and
long-winded; because I'm afraid to pause and wait for the sky to fall
and this planet's green worm to turn

and I write haiku
because my life gets smaller
with every breath

Self-Referential

I was born on a wild and whipping Wednesday in the wake of ambivalent winds. I was born listening to the sweet suckling of lambs. I was born with a caul and a calling.

Small as an atom, beating against hard glass, I was born with a shrunken head and a load of lovely fears, under Virgo and sapphire, in the maternity of modernity.

I was born green with analysis, with pomp and poems, and the ties that blind. Child of Pushkin and Pasternak; cold as Siberia, hot blood of Ukraine.

I have hovered between illness and ego, pus and shiver. I've been low girl on the totem pole. I've been something seismic, and cosmic. I've been engorged, entrenched, enjambed,

encumbered. I've scratched your back and you've scratched mine. I've released my birth certificate and my taxes. I've held my bound feet to the fire.

I have basked in the glow of the glare of the spotlight. I've spit blood through gnashed teeth. I have licked myself into a frenzy. I've soldiered on, I've melted down.

I have walked with a full heart and bulging discs. I have made love to damaged men. I've twitched in my fickle and faithless flesh. I've thrashed in my nondescript skin.

Cindy Hochman

I have filed my Summons and Complaint. I've testified at trial. I've been Exhibit A. I've settled my case while the jury was out. I've weighed myself on the scales of justice.

I have woken with a wooden spoon in my mouth. I've dug in, I've bowed out. I've coveted the wine. I've dreamt of diamond ravens beckoning me with their jeweled beaks.

I have walked on rickety sticks. I have seen my lips lose their gloss. I have melted into water, into waste. I've drowned in moot pools. I've sputtered, gagged, tottered,

and guzzled. I've choked on the hellish bones of madness. I have become the calcified bride. I've made plans and heard God sneer. I've watched my country split its seams.

And everywhere I've walked, I've stepped in grief.

Losing My Mother at Age 5

Then God told me to say goodbye. And she was gone in a cloud of blond silk. While I, in all my gingham, spanked the air and sank into the ground. I needed to be rocked, but she was too busy going from crutches to wheelchair to death bed to final home. She was too young and I was too young. Mother, you were a cut finger, a quick departure. Bionic goddess with legs in chains. I can tell you that there really is such a thing as a death glow—the gorgeous marble eyes at the moment they turn to stone, the blue breath, veins pale as grass. Leaving me to stand alone in the twilight's last weaning.

Cindy Hochman

Swan

for Stephanie Emily Dickinson and Rob Cook

My brilliant attorney/poet father—in my mind a cross between Clarence Darrow, Oliver Wendell Holmes, and Atticus Finch—intense lake-blue eyes, crow-black hair, the epitome of Aquarian sensitivity, once told me that *kids can be cruel.*

And they were. Especially when faced with an abnormally pale, rat-sized, slightly off-kilter proverbial ugly duckling sporting outdated high-water pants and an unsightly pre-Madonna mole on her lower right chin. They swiped my peanut butter sandwiches. They hogged all the Oreos that had been placed lovingly in my lunchbox by the beautiful lady who had recently wed my dashing widower dad. And with their grubby, unkind hands they invaded my vulnerable pockets and filched my dollar bills and spare change, leaving only remnants of lint and the scent of post-traumatic desolation. One day they decided to mold something sticky into my already gnarled and knotted hair. My Spanish teacher, *muy guapo,* on whom I had the usual prepubescent crush, had to cut out the mucky sludge with scissors while my face blazed away in various shades of scarlet and my bowels did the Mexican Hat Dance. I don't think I need to add the fact that I was an anal-retentive goody-goody; I sense that I already had you at *proverbial ugly duckling.*

Then, as in most superficial transformations, Ms. Ugly Duckling, though not eradicated, went underground.

At 18, I snipped and clipped that dirty-blond hair until I almost resembled Mia Farrow in *Rosemary's Baby,* and pealing bells went off in my head as I sashayed my newly revamped pixie self through a reckless coven of promiscuous fire. Suddenly my life was all cigarettes, catcalls, caterwauling, and (oh, yeah) college. No corn silk or corn stalks, for I was a purebred Brooklyn wench, tumbling headlong into a pool of poetry and petrol. Merriment and mayhem in bedlam. Mood rings and mood swings in my pink opium den. Tequila Sunrise rainbows through cut-glass mosaics. Mounted black track lights, waft of spiced musk and pungent patchouli, setting the scene for selected readings from the *Kama Sutra*. Naughty girl, bawdy girl, haughty girl. Saturday night *slutting* (Mom's scowling word) on the steamy Bay Road in the fervid glands of summer. The hunks, an embarrassment of riches: miscellaneous pizza boys, Harvard-educated Norwegian tennis coach, the narcissist next door, and friends of a friend of a friend of my boyfriend. Goldilocks strumpet with a penchant for the callow boys— the cougar and her colts (and a Jewish stallion or two). They fed me things: iced red grapes and Godiva truffles doused with sweet liqueur, and they even recouped my beloved long-lost Oreos.

Then, as in most superficial but underground transformations, Ms. Vixen in Venus put away her rubber playthings, kissed all the Georgie Porgies goodbye

and re-crossed her now matronly legs.

Cindy Hochman

Secret

If you tell me your secret—

I will keep it under my derby hat

I will keep it under my green beret

I will tuck it under my satin pillow

I will dissolve it under my hungry tongue

I will mix it with my errant blood

I will shoot it into my impatient veins

I will shoot it up to bloody Mars

I will comb it through my golden hair

I will shove it under my bitten nails

I will place it inside Pandora's box

I will stuff it into my Burberry boots

I will pour it into my vodka flask

I will stick it into the thorn in my side

I will whisper it to myself at the end of the day

I will recite it in my devout prayers

I will lay it down on a wooden bier

I will shape it in my careful hands

and make it into a glorious poem

Microbes

It came on bat's wings and the vultures descended as the earth went stock-still. Instead of hugs and kisses, every cough a symbol. No longer are we allowed to touch fingers and make a noble chain for peace. Now we clasp our over-washed hands and let ourselves feel each other in more elusive ways. These selfsame hands that go on writing our furious and futile songs.

After a groundswell

After a groundswell of a week, vigilant re: moles and holes, clomping around with bloody boots and sunken folds, I want to clear my mind and think only of gnomes. Let's trade skins. You be dimpled and I'll be freckled, and we'll both be speckled, or peckered, or rumpled (though I'd rather be coupled). Let's have social intercourse with our funnymouths.

"The world is a hot and"

The world is a hot and sloppy place, a stewpot of muck and millstone. The weather betrays us, as the sooty flue of government blows useless black smoke into our faces. We are a nation of scoundrels and sock puppets. In backyards across America, mangy dogs bury the Stars and Stripes, remnants of red, white, and blue under partisan gravestones. Here on the beach we sharpen our shovels and continue digging to China.

Cindy Hochman

The Senators (or, Loaded for Bear)

The senators are trampling through this poem like legislative deer caught in the rosebushes. Some are wearing Republican-red coats; others, blue ties in the shape of Vermont. They have flag pins over their lapels, but they pledge allegiance to the bears. Their national anthem is black bear. The state of their union is brown bear. Their vote on climate change is polar bear. Their stance on guns is silence; instead, they cast unanimous *ayes* in favor of winter. The senators waddle single file like a row of German ducklings, orderly but defeated. They sit in sandboxes of mud, with bloody paws and pockets full of dirty money. When recess is called, they pack up their soapboxes and bullhorns, and retreat to various golf courses or corrupt caves.

An Arbitrary List of Words That Come Up In Just About Every Poem

Birds. Crows. Cicadas. Egrets. Tree, wind, grass, sky, sun, rain, snow, star, earth. Memory. Christmas. Mother, Father (assorted uncles). Abuse. Rape. Water, ocean, riverbed, tide. Husband, wife, new boyfriend, new girlfriend. Kiss. Sex. Love, love, love/lover. Eyelids. Breasts. Abuse. Rape. Baby, toddler, teen, son, daughter, Grandpa, Grandma, brooch. Blue/azure, red/crimson. Food, food, food. Strawberries. Blood orange. Shadow. Joy/sorrow/murder. Lost sock in laundry. City, street, town, church. North, south, east, west. Midwest. New York, Chicago, Brooklyn, Paris. Winter, spring, summer, fall. Home. Kitchen. Closet. Backyard. Cats, cats, meow. Cat's meow. Howl. Pandemic. Death. Rebirth/renewal. Moon, moon, moon, moonlight. And moon.

Cindy Hochman

Wanton Moon

Let's begin by revealing the machinations of the moon—her sources and methods, her bare-faced shenanigans, hiding behind a veneer of buff-colored virtue while spinning soliloquies from the whole cloth of the spurious sky. Tonight the moon is all ruddy-faced and duplicitous, a lewd and promiscuous bride, sullying the celestial bed as she swallows you, and winks down at us.

Surreal *Honeymooners* Poem

Do you remember that old joke:
Last night I dreamed I was eating
a giant marshmallow, and when I
woke up, my pillow was gone?
Well, last night I saw a blubbery moon
from behind my sheer white curtains
that held my imagination 'til
midnight, and I dreamed I was
Ralph Kramden, driving a
New York City bus
into the sky.

Cindy Hochman

Silly Frog Song

Don't sit like a frog
sit like a princess ...
—Denise Duhamel

There are two things I know for sure: (1) it is lots of fun to polly wolly doodle all the day; and (2) no matter how much time goes by, Jeremiah is still a bullfrog. This is the first frog poem I've ever written. I am wary of bulging eyes and dissections. Promiscuous frogs leap from lily pad to lily pad. I was this kind of tadpole once. Frogs do not have to be told to go green. Frogs have no use for fancy hats or politicians. Frogs hate French people. I am the frogman—goo goo gajoob. I once shot a frog in my pajamas (and, no, I don't know how he got into my pajamas, but he looked good in them). Do you know how frogs open gift wrapping? They rip it, rip it. There's something I forgot to tell you before: 'tis better to sleep with a frog than with a newt. (I've never slept with a newt, but when I'm happy, I pin my little legs back.) I was lying. He wasn't wearing my pajamas; he was wearing little froggy Speedos (and he looked good in them). Frogs seem comfortable in their amphibian skin. I wish I were comfortable in my own creamy but wretched skin. Frogs, for the most part, are honest brokers. They pay their taxes. Then they croak.

And they always have some mighty fine wine (yes they do!).

The mercurial muse

The mercurial muse is shaped like a sundial
The mercurial muse puts on her mauve lipstick
The mercurial muse is missing her snowshoes
The mercurial muse has invisible footprints
The mercurial muse likes chit-chat and tangents
The mercurial muse hates lawsuits and tantrums
The mercurial muse left this poem 'neath my lashes
The mercurial muse left 5 poems on my pillow
The mercurial muse left 10 poems in my womb
The mercurial muse is nursing her ducklings
The mercurial muse is drowning in feathers
The mercurial muse is missing her antlers
The mercurial muse is missing her mother
The mercurial muse has run out of ink

Cindy Hochman

Blank White Page

White—the color of devils and doves. Under white knuckles, white page turns to rage. Lackluster pigment and general malaise (ghostly demographics). Better to be mottled, dappled, calico, or tartan. No one even remembers the white chickens; just that bloody red wheelbarrow. No lilies here. Try walking on eggshells with muddy feet and a hail-white heart.

The French say "blanc." Jab of white needle at point blank. Blank white page in whitewash. More than a snowflake, less than a glacier.

My white paper: *Angora cat, pearl onions, pallid bride in lingerie and shy white sheets, glass of white wine ...*

Trembling in my white boots, with my pale face. One day they will crack open my platinum head and donate the curdled white matter (each and every blanched cell of it) to science.

... spilt milk, oatmeal (mind already turned to mush), albino children, false teeth, white flag of surrender.

There was nothing pure about the sick white womb that birthed me.

Poet Bio (with heavy sarcasm included)

I was born in 1957 and voted for Dwight D. Eisenhower. I've been published in many online journals. My mouth is dry from the Lithium and my cold veins are gushing warm blood as we speak. I've never been nominated for a Pushcart Prize (or a Pulitzer Prize either). Is it dusty in here or is it just me? My body is a rectangle of tangles and right angles (I believe in geometric expression). But what should I do with this severed arm, Ma? My work has appeared in Iowa and on the Moon. I have translated Sylvia Plath and Ogden Nash into Sanskrit. My mother told me three things: to cross my i's, dot my t's, and stop dressing like a whore. So I became a prudish proofreader. (Remind me to take my Prozac in two hours.) God is not my co-pilot; He's my chauffeur. He drives me to greener pastures while I drink Jesus juice from the wet bar in the back seat. I'm sick of seeing black flies covering the faces of black children. I'm sick of seeing one-eyed cats in cruel cages. I plan to get my Master's degree as soon as this crippling depression passes. I've been translated into Italian, Farsi, and Pig Latin (I've heard that the pigs really squeal when they hear my poems). Last night I dreamt of hearses and amputations. Or maybe it was horses and allegations (REM sleep has terrible acoustics). When I eat strawberries, I blush. When I drink milk, my tongue swells. When I drink wine, I have epiphanies. (Not true—Jewish girls don't get epiphanies; we get matzo ball soup, bad marriages, lousy sex.) My latest chapbook is *Corpus Delecti (Body of Crime)*. I have no idea where the body is buried, but my lawyer says he can get me off. I'm honored to have my work published in this fine journal. Does this bio need to be in the third person? Is it too many words?

Cindy Hochman

My baby crawls

My baby crawls into the pantry searching for things: her ragdoll cat, a fresh white linen diaper, love, and nourishment. That's what babies do. She eats a few Cheerios that have spilled out of the giant yellow box that holds nothing but *O*'s. She eats a few sugar ants that are slogging their way to building a sacred mountain of dirt, and just like those busy builders, my baby follows her own lofty trail; she is a colony unto herself. Her head is full of magpies, blackbirds, robins, and wrens, though she doesn't yet have words for the birds she observes through an unfettered aviary, the not-yet-hatched nest of her sweet mind. All of this is going on while I, her mother, am wielding a quill and doting on anecdotes, narratives, memoirs, and little white lies. Little white lie number one: it's a nondescript black ballpoint pen, not a quill. Little white lie number two: there's not a single ant in the pantry. Little white lie number three: I don't really have a baby.

Root

You have to go to the root of things. Not like bulbs or soil, but times when your mind is a very sad leaf dropping to the bare ground.

I've become afraid of things that grow or thrive—even love.

Unrest is not always political. When a hurricane blows hard through the precious petals they don't come back. It's a sticky wicket.

But sometimes they do, arriving at your feet with bulging blooms from Emily's wild but prissy garden and a fragrance that wafts from Amherst all the way to your neck of the woods. And their sweetness engulfs you (sometimes to the point of overwhelm).

Maybe this time you allow yourself to sniff it, or touch it, or if you dare, to blow through it yourself, just like the hurricane you've been fearing all along.

Maybe this time you learn that the root is always there, even when you are not. You just have to let yourself flourish. You just have to let yourself

fall first.

Cindy Hochman

Nueve Preguntas (9 Questions)[*]

When did I stop leaping through scorched-earth wildfires and blistering infernos?

Why did God put a curse upon my right breast?

Why did I think that gold rings and matrimony was a capital idea?

When did I learn that love does not conquer all? (It doesn't even conquer half.)

When did tubs of Chubby Hubby ice cream become my go-to dinner?

When did I fall from that flimsy tightrope of my own making?

When did my flaxen hair turn to sullen streaks of gunmetal gray?

When did you turn from corporeal skin to utter dust?

When did I (oh, Sweet Jesus) grow a tail?

---

[*] The number 9 in this poem is a reference to the Nine Circles of Hell in Dante's *Inferno*.

Stochastic Thoughts

I'm hungry, I'm full.
I'm hungry, I'm full.

I've misplaced the moon.

Hey, look! I've got a Ferris wheel in my pocket.

Cindy Hochman

Bob's Old Kitchen

for Bob Heman

Bob's old kitchen has no coffee and Bob don't care. Bob's old kitchen has no vodka and Bob don't care. Bob's old kitchen has no vino and Bob don't care. Bob's old kitchen has no beer or corn chips or ripe tomatoes and Bob don't care. Bob's old kitchen sometimes has green bananas, but (you guessed it!) Bob don't care. An aluminum spoon levitates into the torpid air and Bob don't care. A stray steel ladle bops Bob atop the noggin and Bob don't care. Zoom in on an ancient metal-and-cast-iron stove silhouetting Bob's visage up in the phantasmagoric clouds with burners that flip on and off by their lone selves, endlessly. Bob's old kitchen contains: the dimmest of lights, a fridge full of cheese wedges that laugh, laugh, laugh, and a bear that has hibernated for years in there; a drainboard with peek-a-boo cookware; cabinets, colanders, and a calendar from his accountant on the medieval fridge; a can opener for slicing fickle fingers; and pots and pans that sing and dance at ungodly hours all through the night. *Oh, give us your tired, your poor, your Dinty Moore.* And a spatula spanks the sky. Yes, a spatula spanks the sky. A rubber spatula spanks the thumbnail sky in gleeful and giddy homage to Bob's old kitchen. Bob's old windowless kitchen. Bob's centennial kitchen. *Alte Küche.**

---

* "Old kitchen" in German

I Am the Girl (*travel version*)

I am the girl with the *bon voyage* eyes, I am the girl who is waving goodbye, I am the girl with the contraband in her backpack, I am the girl who won't take off her shoes, I am the girl who won't wash her hands, I am the girl who put the tower in your Eiffel, I am the girl who put the Cockney in your bollocks, I am the girl with Stockholm syndrome, I am the girl who sold you that bridge, I am the girl who prays for Ukraine, I am the girl with a boatload of baggage, I am the girl who never leaves home without it, I am the girl who doesn't go very far.

Cindy Hochman

Inner Life (With Sabotage)

This poem will be intentionally vague.

Candlewicks flicker. Chemicals misfire. Crossed wires refuse to untangle.

Sometimes I slip into something less comfortable.

Carousel horses and streetlights make me weep deeply.

My handsome father's death has turned into stilted breath.

My benevolent brother's death is still caught in my throat.

Everyone gives me flowers to fill the fissure between limbs and loss.

And I bury them under layers of, what? Nothing but my own undoing.

A startled and startling voice tells me to go even deeper than this.

Onyx and obsidian wrestle it out with a chest full of white diamonds.

Frankly, my dear, I've had enough of dancing through the murk with my not-so-better angels.

Excuse me while I remove this battering ram from my solar plexus.

Let me open my palms to the hazy sunshine. I promise I will stop shaking soon.

Cindy Hochman

Shout-outs

Большое спасибо (that's "big thanks" in Russian) to the lovely and talented Jen Knox for giving this chapbook a beautiful and spiritually enlightened home, to the equally talented Christopher Shanahan for the amazing cover art (and for his patience with me therewith), and to the awesome staff of Unleash Press for all their hard work and professionalism.

Special thanks to Bob Heman, my dear friend and poetic collaborator, and to Karen Neuberg, my beautiful and wise confidante in poetry and everything else.

I am so utterly thankful for my family and many friends (in the literary community and otherwise) who have encouraged and sustained me, especially during these turbulent years. Although too numerous to name individually, you know who you are, and you also know that I love, admire, and cherish you.

Thanks also to the Facebook folks who endure my often long-winded but hopefully helpful proofreading tips on Mondays. Yes, yes, I promise to get off my lazy butt at some point and collect them into a book for you.

And for the world, I pray for the restoration of health, unity, and peace.

Biography

Cindy Hochman is the president of "100 Proof" Copyediting Services and the editor-in-chief of the online poetry journal *First Literary Review-East*. She has been on the book review staff of *Pedestal Magazine*, and has written reviews for *American Book Review, Clockwise Cat, Home Planet News, great weather for MEDIA*, and others. Her previous chapbooks are *Wednesday's Child* (Bear House Press), *The Carcinogenic Bride* (Thin Air Media), *Habeas Corpus* (Glass Lyre Press), and *The Number 5 Is Always Suspect* (Presa Press), a collaborative chapbook with poet/collagist Bob Heman. Cindy lives, loves, reads, writes, edits, meditates, learns tai chi, studies Russian, and agonizes over politics in Sheepshead Bay, Brooklyn, and despite what she says in the poem "Poet Bio," she has been nominated for a Pushcart Prize.